Soul of New York

A GUIDE TO 30 EXCEPTIONAL EXPERIENCES

WRITTEN BY TARAJIA MORRELL
PHOTOS BY LIZ BARCLAY
ILLUSTRATED BY ABBIE ZUIDEMA

JONGLEZ PUBLISHING

Travel guides

— Soul of New York is dedicated to all of New York's first responders and essential workers; to the New Yorkers who stayed inside and banged on pots from windows to cheer them on; to the New Yorkers who suffered and the many we lost to COVID-19. Those of us who remain will never forget your care and contribution to our great city. We love and miss you. You are the true Soul of New York. —

'QUITE SIMPLY,
I WAS IN LOVE WITH NEW YORK.
I DO NOT MEAN "LOVE" IN ANY COLLOQUIAL WAY,
I MEAN THAT I WAS IN LOVE WITH THE CITY,
THE WAY YOU LOVE THE FIRST PERSON
WHO EVER TOUCHES YOU
AND YOU NEVER LOVE ANYONE QUITE
THAT WAY AGAIN.'

JOAN DIDION

New York City in 30 experiences? An impossible task, I thought. Confounding. Beguiling! In trying to distill my hometown to 30 places, I soon realized that loving this city is just as much about the spaces *between* places – the journey, if you will – as it is about the destinations.

Hence, for this book, I often wrestled more than one location into 'an experience,' just as a New Yorker would sweeten a mandatory trip to the courthouse for jury duty by slurping Pho for lunch at Thái So'n (a very good Vietnamese restaurant on Baxter Street that didn't make the 30 experiences, but which I'm telling you about right here). We New Yorkers are scrappy and stubborn. We try unendingly to bend the city to our will, but the city always wins, and though exasperated, we love it all the more.

As a kid in the 1980s, I grew up exploring Central Park. In the early 90s, I snuck down to SoHo (before it became a shopping mall), even though my mom still thought it dangerous. In the late 90s, I frequented dimly lit downtown restaurants like Lucky Strike with my aunt and uncle, then slipped into nightclubs that for better or for worse are now obsolete. The city is ever-evolving, ingesting itself, changing its size and shape like Alice in Wonderland (go visit her in Central Park). It's perpetually dancing between nostalgia and progress. As the originals are forced out by gentrification and greedy landlords, facsimiles take their place, hoping to beckon us with whiffs of recognition.

It breaks my heart that I cannot send you to certain places that have been lost in the fray, like Antique Boutique or El Quixote in the Chelsea Hotel (where bohemian poets like Bob Dylan and Dylan Thomas and Leonard Cohen lay their heads) because developers are turning it into a luxury spot. But that's New York.

Here, the parade of flesh, fashion, art and commerce on the street is as hypnotic as any Broadway show. Ours is a walking city, so honor that if you can.

It goes without saying that more was left out than included here, but my hope is to steer you into our many layers: old, new, posh and humble; thriving, surviving and starting perpetually over again.

Let New York exhaust you. It will be worth it.

Tarajia Morrell, author

WHAT YOU WON'T FIND
IN THIS GUIDE

- avocado toast
- Broadway recommendations
- places to take an Instagram photo (Be in the moment!)

WHAT YOU WILL FIND
IN THIS GUIDE

- how to eat pizza like a New Yorker (Warning:
  it's controversial)
- where to see how a seminal artist lived and worked
- how to slim your waist without sit-ups
- dumplings hiding behind a cellphone shop
- what to order at a historically 'feminist' restaurant
- where to get a necklace like Carrie Bradshaw's
- where to play tennis in a train station

Due to the pandemic, lots of businesses closed permanently
or have adjusted their hours of operation.
Please check for most current open hours online.

SYMBOLS USED IN
'SOUL OF NEW YORK'

Free

Less
than $20

$20
to $100

More
than $100

First come,
first served

Make
a reservation

So
New York!

Lovely
for couples

NEW YORK

MANHATTAN

QUEENS

BROOKLYN

GOVERNERS ISLAND

ROCKAWAYS

30 EXPERIENCES

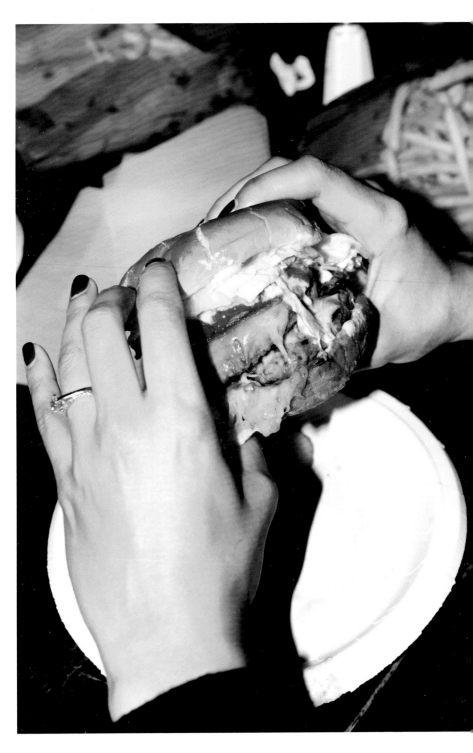

EAT AN
'UNDERGROUND' BURGER

Department stores, the Museum of Modern Art, Rockefeller Center, skyscrapers to spare – there are lots of reasons to visit Midtown. But there's a particular satisfaction to entering the sleek lobby of high-rise hotel The Parker, and seeing a neon beacon while the captivating scent of beef on a griddle guides you toward one of New York's most delicious and unassuming burgers. It's not artisanal here, just the perfect all-American burger in a room that feels like a punk clubhouse bunker.

We love combining high and low, so suggest indulging in a very fancy cocktail at The Grill – the Mies van der Rohe-designed, city-defining restaurant (formerly the Four Seasons) – and then wandering over to the Burger Joint for an all-American classic cheeseburger.

 **THE BURGER JOINT
THE PARKER HOTEL
119 WEST 56TH ST, NEW YORK, NY 10019**

+1 (212) 708 7414   burgerjointny.com

THE GRILL
THE SEAGRAM BUILDING
99 EAST 52ND ST, NEW YORK, NY 10022

+1 (212) 375 9001   thegrillnewyork.com

CUSTOMIZE
YOUR SILHOUETTE

The Lower East Side was once home to countless sewing factories and fabric stores – as well as the immigrants employed by them – and it remains our favorite place to get custom threads.

Gentlemen in need of bespoke suiting head to Freemans Sporting Club, the menswear shop for dignified urban woodsmen that can also fit you for a tuxedo and has a rustically elegant collection of ready-to-wear too. And, yes, Ladies, Freemans' tailors will happily fit you for a suit too!

 FREEMANS SPORTING CLUB
8 RIVINGTON ST
NEW YORK, NY 10002

+1 (212) 673 3209   freemanssportingclub.com

Meanwhile, *Mesdames*: want to tweak your figure but skip the sit-ups? Orchard Corset, which has been supporting women's shapes and augmenting their curves since 1968, is for you. Owner Peggy Bergstein knows your waist size by sight and will cinch at least 4 inches off. Fifty years in, the shop is humble as ever, even though the clientele ranges from celebrities like Madonna and Lizzo to legions of women who want you to think their wasp waist is totally *au naturel*.

ORCHARD CORSET
157 ORCHARD ST
NEW YORK, NY 10002

+1 (212) 874 0786

A MARVELOUS MORNING
IN HARLEM

Let's be real: there is no soul of New York without Harlem and a trip to New York City is incomplete without a visit. The best day to head uptown is Thursday. Make sure to visit the Studio Museum of Harlem, showcasing work by artists of African descent, and the Schomberg Center for Research in Black Culture, in between visits to Harlem's iconic restaurants.

Sylvia's, the famous eatery that's been serving soul food since 1962, is an institution (don't skip a side of the buttery grits), and next door Red Rooster Harlem, chef Marcus Samuellson's bustling ode to the neighborhood's diverse culinary traditions, is boisterous and fun.

SYLVIA'S
328 MALCOLM X BLV
NEW YORK, NY 10027

+1 (212) 996 0660 | sylviasrestaurant.com

CHARLES' COUNTRY PAN FRIED CHICKEN
340 WEST 145 ST (AT EDGECOME)
NEW YORK, NY 10039

+1 (212) 281 1800

But most importantly, visit Charles' Country Pan Fried Chicken, the informal joint in its new location on West 145th Street. Born on a plantation in the South and a New Yorker since 1965, owner Charles Gabriel makes the best fried chicken we've ever tasted. Walk off the sweet potato (obligatory side) stupor by strolling south, past the Apollo Theater and Hotel Theresa, to Harlem Haberdashery to browse their signature clothing line.

EVERLASTING
PIZZA PARTY

We are a pizza town. We've got slice shops aplenty and fancy pizza galore – but there's nowhere quite like Roberta's, the Bushwick restaurant that defines the hipster artists' community from which it grew. At graffiti-covered Roberta's, the woodfire glows onto the picnic tables. It's some of the best pizza and rustic Italian fare one can hope to find, and has a tiki bar and ramshackle garden, to boot. Twelve years in, Roberta's has a 2-Michelin-star restaurant, Blanca, across its back garden and their frozen pies are sold in grocery stores nationwide. Still, eating *morcilla* with pear and a 'Cowabunga Dude' pizza while listening to rock in their rough and tumble dining room is singular to this original spot and cannot be recreated in the privacy of your own home.

ROBERTA'S
261 MOORE ST
BROOKLYN, NY 11206

+1 (718) 417 1118 robertaspizza.com

COURTESY OF ROBERTA'S PIZZA

COURTESY OF ROBERTA'S PIZZA

HOW TO EAT A NEW YORK SLICE

Slice shops, as we New Yorkers fondly call them, are as prevalent and essential to us as our delis: there's pretty much one on every block and they're a cornerstone of New Yorkers' diets, particularly for our late-night rebel rousers. Perfect for a disco dinner before a night of revelry, perfect for an essential snack after a night of drinking, and perfectly adequate for breakfast the next day, our slices are the best way to survive on a budget in this exorbitant metropolis.

But if you want to blend in with the locals, this is how you should master your slice:

(Note: this is a point of controversy.)

NEW YORK CITY'S
VERY OWN SURF TOWN

Our very own beachtown, the Far Rockaways are a car or subway (a train) ride away. We asked local couple, Anna Polonsky (founder of branding studio Polonsky & Friends) and Fernando Aciar (ceramicist and creator of OStudio and O Café), to show us how to Rockaway like pros:

Come to the beach! It's beautiful even in winter!

1. For a great walk, start at Beach 67 and work your way up.

2. Uma's – delicious Uzbeki food!
   92-07 Rockaway Beach Blvd

3. Tacoway Beach* – the spot that made Rockaway famous!
   Surf Club, 302 Beach 87th St

4. Whit's End – brick oven pizza + great grub from local chef Whitney Aycock.
   97-02 Rockaway Beach Blvd (Cash only)

*Open seasonally

5. La Fruteria* – avocado smoothie!
Rockaway Beach Club, Beach 97th St

6. La Cevicheria* – best in town!
97-01 Shore Front Pkwy, Beach 97th St

7. Goody's – top-notch Jamaican food!
7018 Amstel Blvd, Arverne

8. Rippers* – classic burger & rock 'n' roll!
8601 Shore Front Pkwy, Beach 86th St

9. Rockaway Brewing Co. – local beer + cool rotating food
vendors & fun events, etc.
415 B 72nd St, Arverne

10. Rockaway Beach Bakery – don't miss their ham & cheese
croissants and brownies!
87-10 Rockaway Beach Blvd

11. Cuisine by Claudette – we love the banana bread and Açaí bowls!
190 Beach 69th St, Arverne

12. Caracas* – best *arepas* in town!
106-01 Shore Front Pkwy

13.a. Edgemere Farm* – organic produce, honey and groceries!
385 B 45th St

13.b. Edgemere Weekend Market Stand – year round!
3-23 Beach 74th St, Far Rockaway, NY 11692

14. Marina on 72 offers boat rides on bay (go at sunset!)

15. The Castle Rockaway – rooms to rent, events, pop ups,
workshops ++!

*Open seasonally

STAY CALM,
TAKE THE CLASS!

New York City is intense. Whether you live here or have traveled from afar, the city wears on us. The antidote to the crazy is The Class by Taryn Toomey, the perfect way to combat pent-up aggression, release your frustration and tone your bum at the same time.

Founder Taryn Toomey encourages us to be primal, so don't be afraid to grunt or roar and certainly expect to sweat. Supermodels Gisele Bundchen and Christy Turlington are fans of The Class, which weaves together elements of yoga, calisthenics, plyometrics and aerobics. Powerful music and Toomey's tough-love vocal coaching guide you through jumping jacks, 'burpies,' deep breathing and more, to clear your heart, mind and body ... preparing us to fight for another day of New York.

THE CLASS
22 PARK PLACE, 3RD FLOOR
NEW YORK, NY 10007

| Registration online | theclass.com | Wear sneakers and get there early $35 |

FEAST ON *BO SSÄM*
WITH FRIENDS

No one has impacted Asian American cuisine *and* contemporary East Village dining like chef-entrepreneur David Chang and his Momofuku empire. The well-sourced, vibrant menu at Momofuku Ssäm is often eaten with one's hands and has accolades up the wazoo. You and six to ten of your pals can taste why with the *Bo Ssäm* feast: a slow-cooked 7-pound pork shoulder, glistening with brown sugar glaze eaten in *ssäm* wraps with oysters, kimchi, Korean barbeque and scallion-ginger sauce and washed down with bottles of Riesling and Gamay and laughter.

PRO TIP: Get a bunch of friends together and opt for the large-format feasts (pork, duck or crab). Begin your meal with the aged ham flight with coffee-*sriracha* mayo.

 MOMOFUKU SSÄM BAR
89 SOUTH STREET, PIER 17
NEW YORK, NY 10038

+1 (212) 254 3500   ssambar.momofuku.com

A CINEMA
UNLIKE ANY OTHER

Native New Yorker Alexander Olch had a dream: to create a sexy cinema that would reinvigorate the movie-going experience with a bit of Old Hollywood glamour. A visit to Metrograph is the manifestation of that dream.

On any given night, Metrograph screens films essential to the cinematic lexicon, whether instant contemporary classics or forever favorites; historic masters – Godard, Preminger, Wilder and Kubrick – to current game changers, like Noah Baumbach and Spike Jonze. Everything shown at Metrograph is chosen with purpose and projected on 35mm film, the artform's original medium (unless the movie was shot digitally).

Metrograph epitomizes what's great about New York – an ever-evolving city with characters who preserve culture to assure we have a textured future.

PRO TIP: Concession stand before the movie, Metrograph Commissary after.

METROGRAPH
7 LUDLOW ST
NEW YORK, NY 10002

+1 (212) 660 0312   metrograph.com

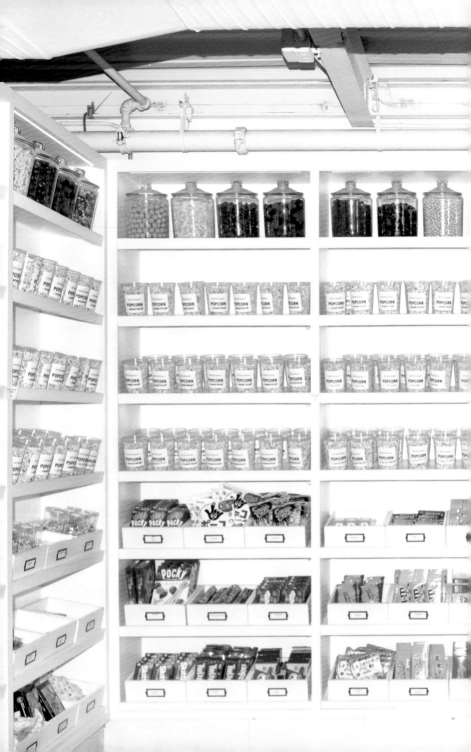

WILLIAMSBURG
PUNCH LIST

If you want to stay in Brooklyn, there's nowhere better than the Wythe, the original Williamsburg hotel in a converted 117-year-old factory building. You don't have to be a guest to enjoy its two restaurant-bars, Lemon's and Le Crocodile, but with their excellent food and sexy scenes, they help to make the Wythe a heavenly place to rest your head.

Time spent in Williamsburg must include a drink and a snack at Achilles Heel in Greenpoint, one of the world's most perfect bars. Have a steam, sauna and massage at Bathhouse. Scavenge at vintage emporium Beacon's Closet, or for a more curated collection, visit bohemian mecca Narnia Vintage. Catch an unusual musical show in a one-of-a-kind structure at National Sawdust or a concert at the Union Pool. Book ahead for dinner at exceptional Italian, Lilia (get the *Mafaldini!*), or Michelin-starred natural wine bar, The Four Horsemen (also a fantastic place for lunch). No reservations? Head to Diner, the restaurant that was here before all the rest. Still raring to go? Hit Baby's All Right for live music and frisky vibes.

 WYTHE HOTEL
80 WYTHE AVE
BROOKLYN, NY 11249

+1 (718) 460 8000   wythehotel.com

NATIONAL SAWDUST
80 NORTH 6TH ST
BROOKLYN, NY 11249

+1 (646) 779 8455

nationalsawdust.org

BATHHOUSE
103 N 10TH STREET
BROOKLYN, NY 11249

+1 (929) 489 2284   abathhouse.com

NARNIA VINTAGE
672 DRIGGS AVE
BROOKLYN, NY 11211

+1 (212) 979 0661   narniavintage.com

LILIA
567 UNION AVE
BROOKLYN, NY 11222

+1 (718) 576 3095   lilianewyork.com

COURTESY OF THE JANE HOTEL

COURTESY OF THE JANE HOTEL

THE TINIEST HOTEL ROOM WITH HISTORY
IN NEW YORK

Sure, the Carlyle, Bowery and Greenwich hotels are swanky, if you've got the funds, but if you've got 'more dash than cash,' there's no better place to stay than The Jane: a former seaman's sanctuary in the heart of the West Village near the Highline and the Whitney Museum. In 1912, survivors of the *Titanic* rested their weary heads here and in the 1980s and 90s, The Jane was the epicenter of bohemian culture and rock 'n' roll rebellion. Now, it's the grooviest spot for travelers on a budget, with tiny bunk rooms that mimic ships' cabins. Communal bathrooms let you befriend a stranger while you brush your teeth, and though the rooms are tiny, the Ballroom hosts some of the most stylish soirées in downtown Manhattan.

THE JANE HOTEL
113 JANE ST
NEW YORK, NY 10014

+1 (212) 924 6700   thejanenyc.com

COURTESY OF THE JANE HOTEL

OH, WHAT A
PERFECT DAY!

A. PERFECT DAY #1, DOWNTOWN-WESTSIDE

Eat a 'Bodega' sandwich for breakfast at High Street on Hudson;
walk the Highline up to Chelsea and zigzag the galleries
between 18th and 26th Streets. Wander down 9th Avenue to
West 10th Street, stop by CAP Beauty Daily for all your natural
beauty and wellness products. Lunch at Via Carota, then swing
by Stonewall to pay homage to those who fought for gay rights.
Wander to Washington Square Park to watch the parade of
musicians, students and dogs frolic. Say 'hi' to Sylvette, a Picasso
between two I. M. Pei towers. For incredible and aspirational vintage, stop by What Goes Around Comes Around in SoHo before
dinner at Frenchette.

FRENCHETTE
241 W BROADWAY
NEW YORK, NY 10013

+1 (212) 334 3883

frenchettenyc.com

B. PERFECT DAY #2, THE EAST VILLAGE & LOWER EAST SIDE

Begin with breakfast pastries and coffee at Abraço. Then, if you love books, stop by Dashwood Books on Great Jones Street or visit Bonnie Slotnick Cookbooks for the astounding collection of culinary volumes in her Lilliputian shop. Need gifts for friends back home? Pop by John Derian on East 2nd Street and then wander down the Bowery to the New Museum for some contemporary art. Thirsty? Head to the bar at Freemans for a cocktail at the restaurant that started the international taxidermy and Edison lightbulb décor craze. For dinner, hit up natural wine bar Wildair and then go on to the Ten Bells if you need more vino. Late night jukebox, pool and cocktails at dive bar Lucy's on Avenue A.

DASHWOOD BOOKS
33 BOND ST A
NEW YORK, NY 10012

+1 (212) 387 8520   dashwoodbooks.com

CHEFS: IÑAKI AIZPITARTE, JEREMIAH STONE (CONTRA, WILDAIR & PEOPLES), PAUL BOUDIER

12

SHOP LIKE
NYC'S BEST CHEFS

New York is the ultimate urban jungle, but the farmers who work tirelessly beyond our city limits are the heroes of our food culture, supplying our best chefs – and many faithful residents – with outstanding products. Heritage pork, hormone-free chicken, fairytale eggplants, pluots in July and tatsoi in December ... we get it all here at the Union Square Greenmarket, founded in 1976 and still thriving today.

Until the 'farm to table' movement in the '70s, Americans considered it a sign of privilege to eat *whatever* they wanted *whenever* they wanted it. Eating locally and seasonally were hallmarks of those who couldn't afford to be choosey. Now the proverbial tables have turned, and it's the wealthy and educated who are privileged enough to consume the best produce at peak season, grown and raised responsibly.

 UNION SQUARE GREENMARKET
UNION SQUARE
MANHATTAN

grownyc.org

LISTEN TO LIVE JAZZ
WITH THE GHOST OF MILES DAVIS

If the walls of the Village Vanguard could talk, they'd whisper tales of the legends who have played there since it opened in 1935. Miles Davis, Thelonious Monk, Charles Mingus, Stan Getz, Bill Evans and many more have graced the tiny West Village basement with their improvised, mesmerizing compositions.

THE VILLAGE VANGUARD
178 7TH AVE S
NEW YORK, NY 10014

+1 (212) 255 4037   villagevanguard.com

THE ICONIC
ARCHITECTURE

THE BROOKLYN BRIDGE

THE UNITED NATIONS

THE GUGGENHEIM MUSEUM

THE OCULUS

THE CHRYSLER BUILDING

THE EMPIRE STATE BUILDING

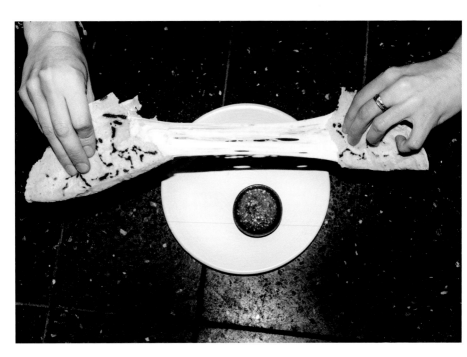

#14

A PHILOSOPHICAL CONSIDERATION
OF 'BRUNCH'

Brunch has come to connote excess in a uniquely American way. But for us – and for Atla – brunch is more about pleasure than countless Bloody Marys; more about a perfect burger or bowl of pasta than eggs-ten-ways, Bellinis and a daytime party. City brunch ideally involves a romantic bike ride or a walk hand-in-hand with a lover to eat a simple meal of shared dishes and to flirt, drinking a bit of wine before going to see some art or a film. If it's not with a lover, 'weekend lunch,' as we prefer to call it, is still an opportunity for indulgence with great friends, the punctuation mark on an afternoon of gossip, sightseeing, vintage shopping and leisure. It's not an excuse to lose a whole glorious Saturday or Sunday to day drinking.

EAT *OMAKASE*
MADE BY AN ECCENTRIC

One of New York's best *omakase* experiences is not where you'd expect it. First of all, it's in Chinatown. Secondly, there's an adjacent *izakaya* and cocktail bar, Straylight, beneath it, where acclaimed artists Jonah Freeman and Justin Lowe have created an immersive, trippy experience inspired by 'art brut.'

But even as a standalone, chef Kazuo Yoshida's *omakase* bar Juku is worth a visit. A larger-than-life personality with a penchant for glitzy street-style labels and dying his hair neon, Nagasaki native Yoshida will lead you through a superb ballet of bites, from amberjack, spotted sardine and *toro* to a vertical tasting of *uni*, his favorite. And if he offers you a taste of something unusual – say, perhaps, cod *semen* – the answer should always be YES.

Trust Kazuo.

 JUKU
32 MULBERRY ST
NEW YORK, NY 10013

+1 (646) 590 2111   jukunyc.com

THE MAGIC TRIO
OF CHINATOWN

Oh, Chinatown, with your sidewalk offerings of squid and durian; your ageless characters spitting endlessly onto the pavement; your massage parlors, Chinese malls and, of course, restaurants. No visit to New York City is complete without a wander through these sticky streets, lived in for centuries by immigrants who flocked here on the wings of dreams of better lives. Chinatown offers velvet Chinese slippers, endless Asian *tchotchkes*, fake Gucci and Louis Vuitton bags, and some of the best food in the city. Royal Seafood, Golden Unicorn, Oriental Garden and Jin Fong are all great bets, but our perfect trio must include lunch at Dim Sum Go Go, a head massage and styling at Mian Tian Hair Salon and some bling at New Top Jewelry.

 DIM SUM GO GO
5 E BROADWAY
(BTWN CATHERINE ST & CHATHAM SQ)
NEW YORK, NY 10038

+1 (212) 732 0797   dimsumgogo.com

- Dim Sum Go Go essentials: duck, mushroom, jade, three star and shrimp–chive dumplings; turnip cake; chives with honey-glazed walnuts. Great for a group.

- At Mian Tian Hair Salon (170 Canal Street, 2nd floor), try the 'Shampoo/Blow/Style' ($15–25) for a 10-min. shoulder/neck massage, 5-min. chair shampoo massage, 10-min. sink shampoo massage, blow dry/style.

- The cool kids flock to New Top Jewelry for 'name' necklaces, à la Carrie Bradshaw, the perfect hoops and charms. Tell Jane we sent you.

 NEW TOP JEWELRY
185 CENTRE ST
NEW YORK, NY 10013

+1 (212) 226 8159

PLAY TENNIS
IN A 107-YEAR-OLD TRAIN STATION

It's essential to visit Grand Central Station, the exquisite Beaux-Arts midtown wonder of architecture and engineering. Admire its reverse Zodiac dome and hunt for its mysterious whisper chamber, but then, why not go play tennis on the little-known courts on the 4th floor?

The Vanderbilt Tennis Club resides in a space that from the 1920s to the 1950s was home to the Grand Central Art Galleries, founded by painter John Singer Sargent among others. Now there are two courts (one regulation size, one junior) on which anyone can play.

 VANDERBILT TENNIS CLUB
15 VANDERBILT AVE (4TH FLOOR)
NEW YORK NY 10017

+1 (212) 599 6500
Reservations only

vanderbilttennisclub.com

THE MOST 'APPETIZING' RESTAURANT
IN NEW YORK

In 1935, founder Joel Russ made a bold move: with no sons, three daughters and a thriving business, he made his daughters full partners and christened the family shop 'Russ & Daughters' – the first American business to have '& Daughters' in its name.

Now, 106 years in, fourth-generation family members Josh Russ Tupper and Niki Russ Federman are *still* teaching New Yorkers (and many visitors) what 'appetizing' means. They've expanded from the cherished storefront at 179 Houston to Russ & Daughters Cafe on Orchard Street (with outposts at the Brooklyn Navy Yard and Jewish Museum uptown too). The sublime cafe is adored for its housemade traditional Jewish cuisine with inventive flourishes. We prefer to skip the long lines at brunch in favor of weekday meals and romantic dinners of borscht, lox and, most importantly, Super Heebsters.

 **RUSS & DAUGHTERS CAFE**
127 ORCHARD ST
NEW YORK, NY 10002

+1 (212) 475 4880 ext. 2   russanddaughterscafe.com

- JOSH RUSS TUPPER & NIKI RUSS FEDERMAN -
FOURTH-GENERATION OWNERS OF RUSS & DAUGHTERS,
THE FIRST BUSINESS IN AMERICA TO ADD '& DAUGHTERS' TO ITS NAME

You say your food category is 'appetizing,' But what does that mean?

NIKI: 'Appetizing' is literally a taste of New York. It's a tradition that started with Jewish immigrants who landed here; it stayed in New York. The word got lost, but we've worked hard to reintroduce it; it's specific to New York.

JOSH: Appetizing is the sister food tradition to delicatessen. Deli is meat, and appetizing is dairy and cured and smoked fish. Appetizing is the food you put on a bagel!

At 106 years old, Russ & Daughters is an indelible institution, but maintaining a successful family-owned business in NYC is so hard. Was there ever a moment when you wondered if you wouldn't make it?

J: There's always that moment. There's always a curveball. Particularly when we committed to opening a restaurant when we didn't know anything about opening a restaurant!

N: Failing is not an option. There's the weight of responsibility of previous generations and our

customers – New Yorkers. We didn't want to be the generation to mess it up. But we just keep looking back to that store on East Houston Street as the reference point for everything we do. We grow from there, so it's authentic and makes sense.

J: It's the long game.

Neither of you planned to go into the family business. Why did you?

N: I grew up appreciating that there was something very special happening in that store. Wherever I went in the world, if Russ & Daughters came up in conversation, the person's face lit up and they'd tell me their story about why Russ & Daughters is important to them. To feel the emotional impact that this place has on people, I realized it was something rare and that I wanted to continue that legacy.

What place or experience evokes the 'Soul of New York' for you?

J: The Freemans bar from 2003 to 2006, 6pm on Wednesdays, when Yana was bartending.

N: Jeremiah Stone and Fabian von Hauske, the chefs from Contra and Wildair across Orchard Street. Their trajectory here in this neighborhood, their success, what New York is to them, the potential for people to live out their dreams. The New York Story.

BEMELMANS BAR
THE CARLYLE (ENTER ON MADISON AVE)
35 EAST 76TH ST
NEW YORK, NY 10021

+1 (212) 744 1600   rosewoodhotels.com

DIVE INTO A MARTINI ...
AND A CHILDREN'S BOOK

There's a pang of anticipation every time we enter Bemelmans, the illustrious Art Deco bar at the Carlyle Hotel with the only remaining public murals by Ludwig Bemelmans, illustrator of the *Madeline* children's books.

Will the waiter procure us a table? Who will we run into?

Soon we've taken a sip of a mammoth martini and our hearts flutter with anticipation as the pianist sits and begins to play. We like to be here just as he arrives (5.30pm, daily) so that we can experience this private thrill. As the music and drink take effect, we observe our surroundings: preppy Upper East Siders, socialites with plastic faces, dignitaries and an occasional celebrity or strumpet. There's laughter, chatter and the tinkling of glasses, but most importantly, the songs reverberating off the storied golden walls.

GIFT LIKE
A NEW YORKER

Paula Rubenstein has a knack for finding gems, one-of-a-kind treasures that a less savvy scavenger might overlook, so luckily for us, she does the searching. Her eponymous Christie Street shop is a cave of wonders where one can hunt for antiques – paintings, textiles, furniture, books and curiosities – that tell stories with their pretty patina.

John Derian Company on 2nd Street is a one-stop shop for New Yorkers in search of the perfect gift. Derian carries the cult French ceramics line Astier de Villatte and represents artist Hugo Guinness, whose whimsical prints are collected by fashionable

PAULA RUBENSTEIN
195 CHRYSTIE ST
NEW YORK, NY 10002

+1 (212) 966 8954   paularubenstein.com

JOHN DERIAN COMPANY
6 EAST SECOND ST
NEW YORK, NY 10003

+1 (212) 677 3917

johnderian.com

locals. But it's Derian's own line of découpage paperweights, plates and trays with images from 18th- and 19th-century nature catalogues and ephemera that are the shop's signature.

Coming Soon is the delightfully eccentric brainchild of owners Fabiana Faria and Helena Barquet, who use their curatorial eye to astutely stock handmade ceramics, colorful carpets, vintage furniture and home goods. Terrazzo planters, pastel milk glass cups, incense and cheeky jewel-toned objects are all here for those with a contemporary aesthetic.

 COMING SOON
53 CANAL ST
NEW YORK, NY 10002

+1 (212) 226 4548   comingsoonnewyork.com

VISIT DONALD JUDD'S
CREATIVE WORLD

With its luxury shops, boutique hotels and bustling restaurants, it's hard to imagine SoHo as a quiet wasteland where artists and squatters resided in former factory buildings and crime ran rampant. Now, few artists can afford to live in this tiny area. But in 1968, the seminal 20th-century artist Donald Judd bought 101 Spring Street for $68,000 as a space in which to live and work.

Donald Judd's Home and Studio is a time capsule that offers not only a rare look into his tranquil and meticulously preserved creative space, but also shows how he lived with his craft and the art of his contemporaries. Moreover, it reveals the ongoing pattern of how our neighborhoods evolve from industrial areas to creative hubs repurposed by artists, and then on to complete gentrification. It's a fascinating trip through time, toil, inspiration and success.

 DONALD JUDD FOUNDATION
101 SPRING ST
NEW YORK, NY 10012

By appointment only	juddfoundation.org/visit/new-york	$25 per person $15 students & seniors, with valid ID

 # 22

RETRO-QUIRKY,
THAI AMERICAN DINER

Our pulse quickens when we arrive and hear the retro Thai soundtrack.

When former fine dining chef couple Ann Redding and Matt Danzer opened Uncle Boons, their Michelin-starred restaurant inspired by the traditional Thai recipes of Redding's roots, they hoped it would be a success, but nothing could have prepared them for the deserved devotion of Boons' fans. Uncle Boons closed during Covid, but the flock has migrated down the street to their new all day spot, Thai Diner.

Folks line up outside for a chance to nosh on fried chicken laab, spicy chopped chicken liver, massaman neuh and khao soi, all eaten with beer slushies, fun wine and cocktails in a quirky, merry atmosphere. It's a winning combination to be finished off with a Thai Coconut Sundae.

 **THAI DINER
203 MOTT ST
NEW YORK, NY 10012**

+1 (646) 850 9480   thaidiner.com

88

POETRY SLAM
SOIRÉE

Beatnik poet laureate Allen Ginsberg called Nuyorican 'the most integrated place on the planet' for good reason. When another skyscraper changes our skyline and it seems that old New York – the real New York – is fading, losing its grit and becoming too shiny and new, it's time to visit the East Village's Nuyorican. On open mic night at this intimate and historic haunt, artists of all races and ages bravely bare their souls through song, spoken word and hip-hop performances, while the audience snaps and claps their support.

In a city where commerce and capitalism are often prized before creativity and authenticity, Nuyorican is one of the most life-affirming experiences out there. Plus you might discover the 'Next Big Thing' before the rest of the world catches on.

NUYORICAN
236 EAST 3RD ST
NEW YORK, NY 10009

Tip: Purchase tickets ahead online as the venue fills up! | +1 (212) 780 9386 | For showtimes and to book ahead, check on the website nuyorican.org

THE CHARM
OF CENTRAL PARK

Central Park is Manhattan's heart. In our concrete jungle, we pine for greenery, away from the noise, traffic and chaos of our towering hive.

Though designers Frederick Law Olmsted and Calvert Vaux began work on the park in 1857, it took nearly 20 years to complete and meant displacing entire villages in what was then mostly farmland. Such is the New York story!

In summer we flock to Sheep Meadow to sunbathe, and in winter we trudge to the rink to ice skate. But it's how the park is present in our everyday – to walk with a pal or dog; to picnic with a date; to see music or Shakespeare; to find some peace and quiet – that most makes us treasure those 843 green acres.

For some of our favorite places to wander or run past while we reflect, turn the page ...

CENTRAL PARK
FROM 59TH STREET TO 110TH STREET
AND BETWEEN 5TH AVENUE AND
CENTRAL PARK WEST, MANHATTAN

CENTRAL PARK.

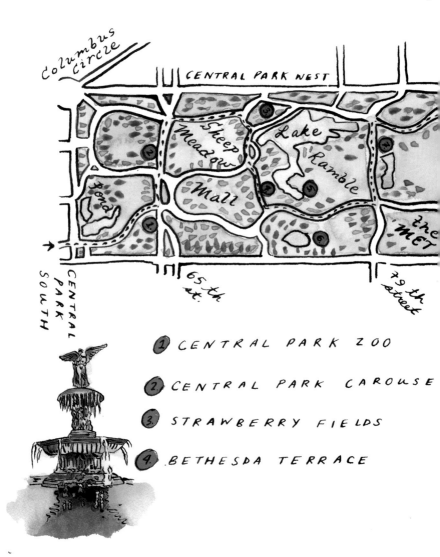

Columbus Circle

CENTRAL PARK WEST

Sheep Meadow

Lake

Ramble

Pond

Mall

the MET

CENTRAL PARK SOUTH

65th st.

79th street

1. CENTRAL PARK ZOO

2. CENTRAL PARK CAROUSE

3. STRAWBERRY FIELDS

4. BETHESDA TERRACE

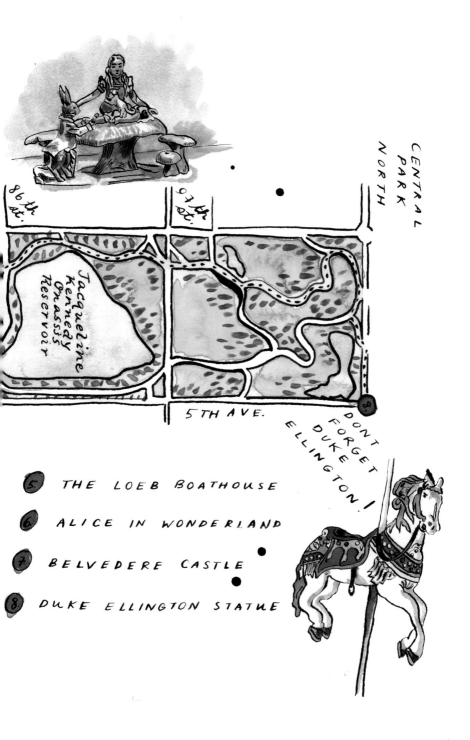

86th. st.

91th st.

Jacqueline Kennedy Onassis Reservoir

5TH AVE.

DONT FORGET DUKE ELLINGTON!

5. THE LOEB BOATHOUSE

6. ALICE IN WONDERLAND

7. BELVEDERE CASTLE

8. DUKE ELLINGTON STATUE

HOW TO HACK
BEING A TOURIST

- It's a myth that New Yorkers aren't friendly. Don't be afraid to ask for directions.

- Look up! So much of the city towers above us. Don't get stuck with your nose in your phone.

- Visit the Metropolitan Museum of Art at night. It's open until 9pm on Fridays and Saturdays ... and prioritize the Egyptian wing.

- The Guggenheim Museum is open until 8pm Saturday through Tuesday and is free from 5pm to 7.30pm on Saturdays.

- The art galleries in Chelsea are closed on Sundays and Mondays.

- If you must go to the top of the Empire State Building, go *after* dinner. The 'City That Never Sleeps' sparkles brightest at night and the last elevator up is at 1.15am, 365 days a year.

- Skip a visit to the Statue of Liberty in favor of a boat ride in the New York harbor from which you can get a great view of Our Lady and of the city. An ideal destination is the LMCC's Arts Center, the new contemporary studio and exhibition space on Governors Island, which is open seasonally and accessible by ferry.

- Ferries are our friends: water taxis connect the boroughs, give respite from the bustle of mass transportation and there's never any traffic.

- Yoga for the People offers $10 classes.

- Eat at our best restaurants at lunchtime (Le Bernardin, Cosme, Casa Mono ...)

- Citibikes are great. Stay in your lane and don't go against the traffic.

- At Grand Central Station, look up at the constellations on the Beaux-Arts ceiling. In the northwest corner of the dome, you'll see a darker square, which was left after the ceiling was cleaned to show patrons the damage a century of soot had done.

THE ISAMU NOGUCHI FOUNDATION AND GARDEN MUSEUM
9-01 33RD RD (AT VERNON BLVD)
LONG ISLAND CITY, NY 11106

+1 (718) 204 7088   noguchi.org

HOW TO CONQUER
QUEENS

There are so many reasons to fall in love with Queens. Twenty minutes from Midtown Manhattan, in Long Island City, MoMA PS1 is one of America's largest institutions dedicated to contemporary art. But for a tactile, serene and captivating experience, nothing compares to the Isamu Noguchi Foundation and Garden Museum, where there are rarely crowds and you can walk among the pioneering Japanese artist-designer's works in stone, wood, brass and, of course, paper.

Do not leave Queens without eating. Jackson Heights is one of the most multicultural experiences in the world, let alone New York City. There are approximately 6,000 restaurants in Queens (emblematic of the 120 nationalities that reside in this borough) and 'Little India' (74th Street off Roosevelt Avenue) has a particularly diverse selection. Follow a passageway between two cellphone shops to unassuming Lhasa Fast Food for beef and chive *momos* (South Asian dumplings) and myriad other spicy Tibetan delights.

MOMA PS1
22–25 JACKSON AVE
LONG ISLAND CITY, NY 11101

+1 (718) 784 2086

moma.org/ps1

LHASA FRESH FOOD
81-09 41ST AVE
QUEENS, NY 11373

+1 (917) 745 0364

LHASA

But the essence of what we love about eating in New York is at Dawa's in Woodside, where chef Dawa Bhuti combines her Himalayan heritage with the impeccable sourcing ethos she learned while cooking at upscale NYC restaurants.

 DAWA'S
51-18 SKILLMAN AVE
WOODSIDE, NY 11377

+1 (718) 899 8629   dawasnyc.com

COURTESY OF THE ODEON

THE THEN, NOW, &
HOPEFULLY FOREVER
NYC RESTAURANT

In 1980, three restaurateurs – brothers Keith and Brian McNally and Lynn Wagenknecht – who would each go on to open some of the city's most beloved eateries and wateringholes, conceived of New York's perfect brasserie in a former 1930s cafeteria.

Frequented by creatives (Basquiat, Warhol, Calvin Klein, Madonna and DeNiro, to name a few) and memorialized in Jay McInerney's *Bright Lights, Big City*. The Odeon defined a cocaine-fueled era of excess. Though the vibe has mellowed considerably, the restaurant remains a beacon of our city that's flourished through fads and floods. With something for everyone on the menu, it's less a place for tourists than a neighborhood anchor and destination for true New Yorkers. Let's hope we can visit for another forty years.

THE ODEON
145 W BROADWAY
NEW YORK, NY 10013

+1 (212) 233-0507

- ADAM PLATT -

Adam Platt is *New York Magazine*'s restaurant critic and for two decades has been sharing the trials, tribulations and delights of dining in our city and the merits of our food culture. Platt recently released *The Book of Eating*, a memoir about growing up in Hong Kong, Tokyo and France, and eventually becoming our most sardonic and amusing critic.

What do you think about our food-obsessed city?

In New York, there's an old dining culture, and you discover quickly that going out to restaurants is not just done occasionally but all the time. The family-togetherness meal is often something done in a restaurant. New Yorkers have this innate questing desire to discover and go to places, old and new, in a variety of different styles. New York has always been obsessed with what's in fashion, being in the know ... not just the best new French restaurant, but the most prosaic thing – the best pizza, ramen, burger – as the end of fine dining and beginning of millennial chef culture. What's been in fashion in terms of food for the last 15 to 20 years is the stuff that chefs are obsessed with: ingredients, technique, simplicity, innards, whatever the hell.

What makes New York a unique eating destination?

It's the combination of the three key things that make New York unique: the depth of dining culture; the variety of styles; and the close proximity and busyness that's the essence of life here. The depth of dining culture exists in Tokyo and Paris and any Italian city, but they don't have the variety. In LA you have great variety, but you don't have the dining culture. Here, it may not be the best Chinese, Malaysian or Mexican food in the world, but there are few places in the world where you can take a journey from borough to borough and taste the entire world. New York is the one place where you can often literally stay in one neighborhood and the world will come to you.

The variety is a reflection of the tapestry of New York

What's New York's terroir?

New York is a meat and potatoes town. The terroir of New York dining is an oyster and a piece of steak. The pizza slice, knish, bagel or hot dog, it's something that you do on the fly. It's something that's portable, something that meshes with the frenetic busyness of the city. Our versions are durable to survive the rigors of a New York day on the move; relatively cheap and reliably delicious with primary flavors and umami, stuff that cuts through the chaos.

What would you say is an iconic New York dish or dining experience?

My answer has always been the Grand Central Oyster Bar because it's in this nexus of movement and travel but everyone's moving and going somewhere, and oysters are our terroir food, but it's gotten so bad lately.

Le Bernardin is a great neighborhood restaurant. Like all great New York restaurants, they function as neighborhood restaurants. It's the neighborhood restaurant for the midtown power older crowd. Run by a family. Chef is there – he's from somewhere else but he's undisputedly a New York chef, who stays at his restaurant. You can't go there and not feel a sense of the grandeur of the city. If you want to feel the grandeur of New York, go to a late lunch at Le Bernardin.

 # 27

EIGHTY-EIGHT ICE CREAM FLAVORS (AND SOME FIZZES)

Imagine being such an ice cream fanatic that you feel compelled to offer seven versions of vanilla, six takes on chocolate, five caramels, five coffees and five strawberry flavors ... plus utterly unique combinations such as pistachio shiso, banana curry and salt & pepper pine nut!

Lucky for us that Nicholas Morgenstern is that ice cream obsessive. His Greenwich Village flagship offers 88 flavors, using impeccable ingredients free of any additives, plus has a sundae bar – where you can also eat an insanely satisfying Morgenstern's burger and fries – and a tiny little cocktail bar. Morgenstern's Fizzy Bubbly, to boot. Basically, Morgenstern's Finest Ice Cream has everything that makes us smile.

MORGENSTERN'S FINEST ICE CREAM
88 W HOUSTON ST
NEW YORK, NY 10012

morgensternsnyc.com

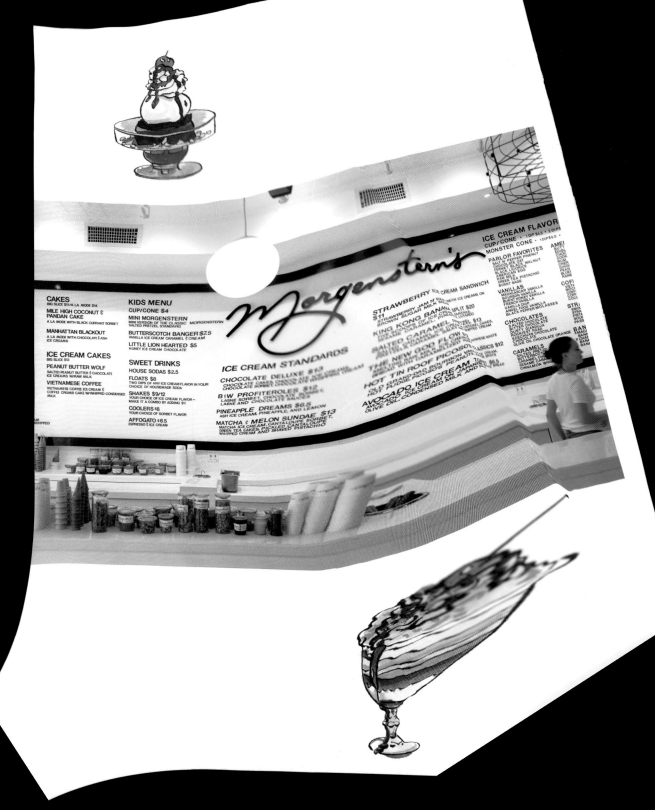

Morgenstern's

CAKES
BIG SLICE $11/A LA MODE $14

**MILE HIGH COCONUT &
PANDAN CAKE**
A LA MODE WITH BLACK CURRANT SORBET

MANHATTAN BLACKOUT
A LA MODE WITH CHOCOLATE & ASH
ICE CREAMS

ICE CREAM CAKES
BIG SLICE $13

PEANUT BUTTER WOLF
SALTED PEANUT BUTTER & CHOCOLATE
ICE CREAMS W/RAW MILK

VIETNAMESE COFFEE
VIETNAMESE COFFEE ICE CREAM &
COFFEE CRUMB CAKE W/WHIPPED CONDENSED
MILK

KIDS MENU
CUP/CONE $4

MINI MORGENSTERN
MINI VERSION OF THE CLASSIC MORGENSTERN
SALTED PRETZEL STANDARD

BUTTERSCOTCH BANGER $7.5
VANILLA ICE CREAM CARAMEL & CREAM

LITTLE LION HEARTED $5
HONEY ICE CREAM CHOCOLATE

SWEET DRINKS
HOUSE SODAS $2.5

FLOATS $8
TWO DIPS OF ANY ICE CREAM FLAVOR IN YOUR
CHOICE OF HOUSEMADE SODA

SHAKES $9/12
YOUR CHOICE OF ICE CREAM FLAVOR—
MAKE IT A COMBO BY ADDING $1!

COOLERS $8
YOUR CHOICE OF SORBET FLAVOR

AFFOGATO $6.5
ESPRESSO & ICE CREAM

ICE CREAM STANDARDS

CHOCOLATE DELUXE $13
CHOCOLATE CAKES, CHOCOLATE ICE CREAMS
CHOCOLATE SORBET

B&W PROFITEROLES $12
LABNE SORBET, CHOICE OF ICE CREAM
LABNE AND CHOCOLATE

PINEAPPLE DREAMS $6.5
ASH ICE CREAM, PINEAPPLE AND LEMON

MATCHA & MELON SUNDAE $13
MATCHA ICE CREAM, CANTALOUPE SORBET,
GREEN TEA CAKES, PICKLED CANTALOUPE,
WHIPPED CREAM AND SHAVED PISTACHIO

STRAWBERRY ICE CREAM SANDWICH
STRAWBERRY JAM N' SODA CREAM ICE CREAMS ON
$11 BROWN SUGAR MILK

KING KONG BANANA SPLIT $20

SALTED CARAMEL

THE NEW GOD FLOW

HOT TIN ROOF PICOSO
OLD GRANDDAD BOURBON VAN
HOT FUDGE PICOSO'S JAM, TON

AVOCADO ICE CREAM
AVOCADO ICE CREAM,
OLIVE OIL, CONDENSED MILK AND

ICE CREAM FLAVOR
CUP/CONE • 1 DIP $4.5 • 2 DIPS $5
MONSTER CONE • 1 DIP $5.5

PARLOR FAVORITES

VANILLAS

CHOCOLATES

CARAMELS

QUICK CUPS
TO-GO
$5
FLAVORS
BURNT HONEY VANILLA
SALTED CHOCOLATE
CARAMEL PRETZEL
GREEN TEA PISTACHIO
SMOOTH & DELICIOUS
STRAWBERRY
SCHOOLYARD
MINT CHIP
CASH
PLEASE KEEP
SERVICE DOOR
CLEAR OF
OBSTRUCTION
AT ALL TIMES
THANK YOU!

PASTRAMI
ON RYE

The drooling begins when we enter Katz's and get our little orange ticket. It's anticipation for the pastrami on rye that we're about to demolish, but it's also for the atmosphere, the energy, the simple joy.

Since it opened in 1888, Katz's has provided great food and a welcoming environment to its community. In the late 19th century, when Jewish immigrants made New York City the Yiddish theater capital of the world, Katz's became their de facto clubhouse and meeting spot. It's been beloved by celebrities ever since (attested to by the kitschy photos on the walls), but it's Katz's authenticity and consistency that have made it endure for New Yorkers.

PRO TIP: The order is simple: pastrami with mustard on rye. It comes with blissfully snappy pickles and while we're at it, we like the coleslaw.

 KATZ'S DELICATESSEN
205 EAST HOUSTON ST
(CORNER OF LUDLOW ST)
NEW YORK, NY 10002

+1 (212) 254 2246   katzsdelicatessen.com

- SYLVIA WEINSTOCK -

LIFE LESSONS FROM A NATIVE NEW YORKER AND BAKER EXTRAORDINAIRE

Where did you grow up?

I grew up in Williamsburg on North 8th Street and Bedford Avenue in a cold-water railroad flat, with no steam heat. I left when I was nineteen and got married. I never go back ... Except the other night, I went to Williamsburg for dinner at the Wythe Hotel. I almost stopped to see the corner of North 8th and Bedford, but I don't believe in going backwards, I believe in going forward, so I didn't stop. That

I like being older, I get away with a lot of nonsense

chapter is over. That's a good trick: learning how to move on.

For how long have you resided in Tribeca?

I've been living in Tribeca since 1983, and I'm not leaving. If I leave, they carry me out of here!

What's your New York like? Your Tribeca?

The city is divided in many ways. There's the Upper East Side, where the sidewalks are nice and smooth, and everyone lives in tall apartment houses and nobody knows each other. Downtown is another story. In this neighborhood, everyone talks to each other on the street, on the elevator. I had an accident about two years ago and was walking with a cane. People would say, 'Can I help you cross the street?' 'Can I carry that package for you?' I find this area comforting. People absorb each other and help each other. They pick each other up. They say, 'I like your coat!'

How has Tribeca changed in your tenure?

These Tribeca lofts were all factories. Then the artists moved here and lived in 5,000 sq. ft lofts for $20 a month rent. Then the owners found that they could get more money, so goodbye, artists! Now you have people paying $15,000 a month rent. Now these lofts are full of young families.

Where do you like to eat?

I eat at home. I cook for chefs – simple stuff, but they are happy to eat in a home and not in a restaurant. I eat nearby as much as I can because I want to support my neighborhood. I go to Odeon, Frenchette, Petrarca. I went to Tamarind the other day. Years ago as a student, you could get a 3-course meal for $1.95. Life was different. There's nothing like nickels anymore.

What was your profession?

I had Sylvia Weinstock Cakes for 40 years and I had an extraordinary run of clientele.

A lot of out-of-towners find New York City extremely intense. What do you say to them?

New York is a high-energy city ... not stressful. It depends on your attitude. The way people walk, the way they talk ... you feel it. We are a liberal city: tattoos up the gazoo that would not function in the Midwest. That's why they left and came here! They gravitate to an area that's accepting and secondly that's exciting.

Is New York still exciting?

Exciting comes from the people you know and your attitude. You could sit in a wheelchair in the corner and prepare to die. Or you can get out there and go to lunch and talk to young people and learn about them ... People are wonderful. Living here is invigorating.

FLOAT AWAY
IN AN ANCIENT BATH

Descending into the Aire Ancient Baths in Tribeca is like entering another dimension. Housed in a former textile factory building built in 1833 with stunning exposed beams and brick, the thermal pool room is dark and soothing, quiet and sensual. It's the perfect place to rejuvenate from the noise and scuttle of the city (and pretend you're in 5th-century Rome), with amenities and treatments comparable to a 5-star hotel.

There are experiences tailored to couples (and indeed couples love to come here together), including a bath in Spanish Ribera del Duero red wine, but our preference is for scrubbing ourselves with sea salt and then floating in the soothing and serene salt water pool.

 AIRE ANCIENT BATHS
88 FRANKLIN ST
NEW YORK, NY 10013

+1 (646) 878 6174

beaire.com
bookingnytribeca@beaire.com

30

THE HOTEL THAT'S A ONE-STOP SHOP
FOR NIGHT-TIME REVELRY

'Where can we go to dance?'

It's the endless New York question. We have two lively and very distinct options for you, both at the Roxy Hotel in Tribeca.

Descending into the subterranean jazz club. The Django, is a transporting experience that will make you think you've arrived in 1920s Paris, where crooners in stylish retro suits serenade you and force your feet to move.

THE ROXY HOTEL TRIBECA
2 6TH AVE
NEW YORK, NY 10013

+1 (212) 519-6600

roxyhotelnyc.com

Meanwhile, at Paul's Baby Grand, the pink-accented lair from nightlife legend, Paul Sevigny, DJs play fun, happy 'goodtime music' from all eras. It's literally the place that Mark Ronson referred to in his song, 'Leaving Los Feliz.' From the dancefloor, you can admire paintings by contemporary artist wunderkind, Josh Smith, which are all over the boîte.

Fun fact: the dapper, white-haired gentleman, Roger, who will make your cocktail was Madonna's first beau when she arrived in New York City in the late 1970s.

PRO TIP: Say my name at the door and you're more likely to gain entry. xo Tarajia.

THE DJANGO
THE ROXY HOTEL TRIBECA
2 6TH AVE
NEW YORK, NY 10013

thedjangonyc.com

PAUL'S BABY GRAND
THE ROXY HOTEL TRIBECA
2 6TH AVE
NEW YORK, NY 10013

roxyhotelnyc.com/dining/pauls-cocktail-lounge

Entry to the lounge is by doorman's discretion

We never reveal the 31ˢᵗ address
in the Soul of series because it's strictly confidential.
Up to you to find it!

SEASONAL
SECRET

We never reveal the name of our 31st experience, but if you find
yourself in an intimate antique wood-paneled bar, then you're
nearly there. We can't tell you what to order, because that's up
to the chef, whose specialty is *kaiseki* – Japanese seasonal dishes
using the best local products. We recommend putting yourself
in his creative hands and enjoying the ride.

 THROUGH 'THE HALL'

Reservations required
odo.nyc

MANY THANKS TO

FANY PÉCHIODAT for giving me the opportunity to fall in love with my hometown all over again.

LIZ BARCLAY AND ABBIE ZUIDEMA for their persistence, generosity and gorgeous imagery that make this book come to life.

THOMAS JONGLEZ for his contemporary take on guidebooks for inquisitive, modern travellers.

EMILIEN CRESPO for the songs, and for suggesting me to Fany and encouraging me to share my New York.

ANNA POLONSKY AND FERNANDO ACIAR for the introductions they make for me to foodies and friends all over the world and for sharing their contribution herein.

NASTASSIA LOPEZ for listening, reading, guidance and friendship.

ADAM PLATT for making me laugh and consider how essential restaurants are to life, even years before we ever met.

SYLVIA WEINSTOCK for sharing her sage wisdom and contagious zeal for life.

MAMA CATHY MORRELL for her support and keen editorial eye.

PAPA PETER MORRELL for showing me how to love restaurants, from diners to fine dining, from Day One.